T0171377

GOD HEALS

JEFFREY M YUNA

WestBow
PRESS
A DIVISION OF THOMAS NELSON

WestBow Press books may be ordered through booksellers or by contacting:

WestBow Press
A Division of Thomas Nelson
1663 Liberty Drive
Bloomington, IN 47403
www.westbowpress.com
1-(866) 928-1240

Because of the dynamic nature of the Internet, any web addresses or links contained in
this book may have changed since publication and may no longer be valid. The views
expressed in this work are solely those of the author and do not necessarily reflect the views
of the publisher, and the publisher hereby disclaims any responsibility for them.

Any people depicted in stock imagery provided by Thinkstock are models,
and such images are being used for illustrative purposes only.

Certain stock imagery © Thinkstock.

ISBN: 978-1-4497-8499-7 (sc)
ISBN: 978-1-4497-8498-0 (hc)
ISBN: 978-1-4497-8500-0 (e)

Library of Congress Control Number: 2013902609

Printed in the United States of America

WestBow Press rev. date: 3/8/2013

CONTENTS

Introduction • vii

God's Will • 1

Faith of the Receiver • 19

Faith of the Prayer • 29

Motives • 37

Demonic Influence • 51

In the Name of Jesus • 67

The Gift of Healing • 79

Testimonies • 83

Acknowledgments • 93

INTRODUCTION

Is there a more controversial subject within the Christian community than healing? After all, whole denominations have pronounced the end of God's healing on earth and subscribe to the belief that He stopped some time shortly after the documentation of the Bible ended. Other denominations take it to the extreme, and would even test God's healing ability and scripture with dangerous, self-debasing acts designed to prove the word true. This says nothing of so many Christians who need physical healing or who would kill to have the gift of healing operate through them. More so, modern day science would have you believe healing outside of the medical establishment or the bodies own natural ability does not exist. Often a miraculous disappearance of symptoms is dismissed as an original false diagnosis or other quirk of fate. The value of prayer in bringing recovery from many illnesses has been acknowledged and documented, yet the lack of **consistent** results seems to be all the proof that is needed for non-believers to argue that healing is not the responsibility of work of the Lord. This book would argue otherwise.

Healing in all its forms is the work of God, and the **consistency** of God's healing is what this book intends to address. The hypothesis, if you will, is that God heals. What the next several chapters will cover is why there are such inconsistent results with prayer and God's healing. With an in depth look at the five aspects of God that are involved in healing you will see that God is not at all inconsistent. God is labeled inconsistent because healings do not occur in every case. Yet in every case God's plan to build a relationship with mankind is the consistent denominator. In reality, God will use five factors to begin, encourage, or grow a relationship with Him.

Exploring God's healing as a tool of relationship requires the consideration of the first factor: God's **will** as it relates to healing. Beyond His will is the basis of the second and third factors: **faith**. The faith of the person doing the praying, and the faith of the person receiving and in need of the healing. The fourth factor of **motivation** must also be considered when looking at the results. Finally, the level of demonic activity that has manifested the situation must also be considered. These five factors, God's will, the faith of the one praying, the faith of the one receiving, the motives of the parties, and the demonic activity all must be considered before declaring the end of healing. When applied to individual instances these factors reveal that God's healing is completely consistent, and not vice versa. When collectively weighed, these factors demonstrate that the Creator of the Universe is not bound by formulas, spells, or the will of man. Rather, God is bound by an unconditional love for mankind that forces Him to promote relationship. God does heal, and He does so as an act of love, as proof of His existence to some, and at His will. Without limitation of time or generation Jesus states in Mark 16: 17- 18 that for the Christian, *"these signs will accompany those who have believed: in My name ... they will lay hands on the sick, and they will recover."* This has occurred throughout history, from the moment Christ left the earth to to-day. I am a first hand witness to this very thing.

The goal and objective of this book is two-fold. For the reader to gain answers and understanding to many questions they have concerning God's healing powers, and secondly to see the same reader walk in a new understanding and to become part of God healing others. The goal is to see testimonies like the following created within the reader as well.

It was an average morning and Cynthia Sisto and I had gone to eat breakfast at Fountain View Café in Houston (yes, I have used names and places, because what use is a testimony without witnesses?) It was a normal morning. Not a particularly spiritual time, in fact it was a breakfast date, if there is such a thing. The only thing remotely spiritual was the fact that I was wearing a bright orange t-shirt that quoted Mark 16: 17-18 on its back. At Fountain View Café every patron waits in line to order before sitting down and Cynthia and I followed in that tradition. After ordering we found a seat in the corner of the restaurant. I can't even remember what it was we had to eat, because frankly my focus and attention was on the lovely young lady keeping my company. While eating there, and playing the flirtatious games that singles will, a man walked up to our table with an extreme stutter.

He said, " x..x..x..excuse me… d.da..da… do..u..u. you…b..b.. ba..believe..th..that…sh…sh..shirt?"

I said, "Not only do I believe this shirt, but I have seen everything on it."

I will forgo the literary genius necessary to try to portray the entire conversation in stutter form and summarize by telling you that the man, in his 40's, had a stroke, with the results being this extreme stutter. He went on to explain that he was very fearful and on his way to the doctor. He was afraid of another stroke as he had recently been experiencing the onslaught of headaches. To my shock he asked us to pray for him.

Emboldened by the Holy Spirit Cynthia and I prayed for the

man right there in the middle of the restaurant. Not sitting quietly at the table mind you. I stood up right there, placed my left hand upon the man and began to pray. What I prayed is irrelevant other than to say I listened for what God would have me pray. At the end of the prayer the man said, "thank you."

Cynthia looked at me, I looked at her and we were shocked. The man did not say, "t..tt.th..thank… y.y.y.y. you." He said, "thank you," crystal clear, and without a stutter. I laugh about it today. He was not even aware that his stuttering had ceased. He acknowledges his headache was gone, but did not have the first clue he was no longer stuttering. In fact, he was a bit perturbed that I was laughing. *No way* was I going to be the one to point it out. As he left to go to his doctor's appointment I gave him a simple command from the Lord. I told him, "I want you to say your ABC's all the way to the doctor." He left acknowledging that he would.

Can you imagine his surprise when he finally realized he was not stuttering? I sincerely hope that he did not wreck his car when the realization hit him. That was a good day, a good moment, and a moment available to all who will believe.

For Cynthia, she discovered God's word was true and though she believed in healing, she experienced it first hand. Her relationship to Christ was forever changed. For the stroke victim, he would soon discover that his hope had become reality. In his healing, I am confident that a new relationship to God was born. For me, I longed for more. This was not a televangelist praying for one person in the midst of thousands. This was a business owner on a breakfast date, approached by a complete stranger with a random question. God had no reason to use me, but because He loves us He saw an opportunity to increase three different relationships. It was a moment when the five factors of healing all lined up to create a miraculous result--factors that will now be explored in detail.

God's Will

God's will comes into play in every healing, and does so in two manners. The first manner can be characterized as God's specific will for an individual. The second manner is God's sovereign will, which is independent of any of the other aspects of the healing process. In other words, God's agenda, His plans and purpose must be not only considered but understood in prayers of healing. God not only knows the number of hairs on every head of humanity, but He knows ultimately what is in the absolute best interest of the individual. God's will is motivated by love and for individual good, therefore that will knows what is ultimately better for the individual. It is entirely possible that not healing a person is more inclined to drawing a person to God that healing them. Outside this will for the individual God has a sovereign will that is completely independent of anything other than His desires, whims, or goals. God can act sovereignly simply because He is God.

In order for any healing to take place it must first and foremost be the will of God. This is to not say that everyone who is not healed didn't receive the gift because God did not want them too. It is simply to say that it should be the first of the five considerations when healing is needed. The notion that "it is the will of God" for someone to die of cancer, stroke, heart attack, or any other manner of disease, is preposterous. Equally preposterous is the notion that God's will is for everyone to be healed. For God, the Creator of the Universe, the One who is motivated by love and far wiser than any man, will never allow Himself to be boxed into a definition. To define His will is to number the stars. It is impossible to comprehend fully. As incomprehensible as His will is, each healing becomes a case-by-case study of the will of the individual in need of the healing. God knows the conditions of the hearts involved. This, when considered by the love of God will always produce the results that are in the best spiritual interest of the parties. God is the master chess player and His board has four billion pieces and 4 billion players. He is not only able to anticipate the individual next move, but He is able to anticipate and predict how each move will influence the next, and what the end of the game will be.

Furthermore, He knows when His intervention will influence the outcome to the positive.

In hundreds, perhaps thousands of visits to the dying there is nary a one who is not concerned with the will of God in their life. There is nary a one who did not ask "why me?" On occasion chance will find a person ready for death, embracing the future with God, but this is rarer than diamonds. On the contrary, God uses the rough circumstances of our lives to draw us to Him. It could be argued no one in the Bible lost more than Job and lived to tell about it. The end however was a greater relationship with God. Job 42:5 culminates this revelation when it says, *"I have heard of Thee by hearing of the ear; BUT NOW MY EYE SEES THEE."* The result of Job losing his physical possessions, family, and health was a new experiential relationship with God. Job had heard *of* God with His ears through the teaching of men. In the end though, he *experienced* God for himself. He came to a subjective knowledge of the person of God that he described as seeing with his eyes. It was God's ultimate purpose for Job to know Him in a new way. God's will, in every case, is for us to know Him. And God is not pressed by human emotions to prevent any hardship or bring any blessing that might bring that end. First and foremost, God desires that we come to know Christ in the act of salvation. Matthew 18:14 says, ***"So it is not the will of Father who is in heaven that one of these little ones perish."*** Salvation plays a huge role in determining God's will in any healing, and is of supreme importance to the Him. We will discover that God is about relationships. However every relationship must have a beginning, and a Christian's initial relationship with God is established in the act of salvation.

Universally, the first question asked in every hospital visit is "where does that person stand with the Lord?" Are they saved? Do they need to repent of unforgiven sin? Is there anything standing in the way of their relationship to God? To the minister the answer is irrelevant, as God will heal the Christian and non-Christian alike. To God and the person in need of healing, the question is of critical importance. As ministers praying for the healing of the sick, ***judgment of a person's spiritual condition*** is not the purpose. But making the person ***consider their own spiritual condition*** is. Bringing God's will of relationship is important to everyone, particularly those in distress. Healing is merely one tool, one gift in the arsenal of God to bring about relationship. Likewise, God knows in advance which will draw a person closer: to receive a healing, or to not. It is this will of God that is so supremely important that it caused Jesus to pray, ***"Thy will be done on earth as it*** *is in heaven."* Without a concern for this will, then the direction of the healing can never be determined.

An excellent Biblical example of the will of God superseding the will of man in the area of healing is found in the story of Lazarus. As a precursor to this story remember the words of Christ in John 5:19 where He says, *"Truly, truly, I say to you, the Son can do nothing of Himself, unless it is something He sees the Father doing; for whatever the Father does, these things the Son does in like manner."* Christ was completely in touch with the Father's will. Because of this the miracle with Lazarus occurred as depicted in John 11. There Mary and Martha, the sisters of Lazarus, come to Jesus with news Lazarus is sick. Verse 3 says, *"...he whom You love is sick."* However, Jesus does not immediately jump up and go to him even though He "loves" him. To the contrary, verse John 11:5-6 informs the reader what happened. *"Now Jesus loved Martha, and her sister, and Lazarus. When therefore He heard that he was sick, He stayed then two days longer in the place where He was."* Could there be a stranger reaction in love? Here Christ has a sick friend whom He admittedly loves, therefore He stays two day longer away from him? Christ knew the will of God in this situation and the love for the people caused Him to remain in that will. The end result was Lazarus's death and ultimate resurrection, but the will of God was none the less in opposition to the will of man and the Son of Man. In fact God's will was so completely opposite that of man's will that verse 35 of the same chapter says, *"Jesus wept"* as he approached the tomb of his friend. Even though Jesus knew that God would raise His friend from the dead, Jesus cried. He cried in part because His will and desire was to immediately satisfy His friends in their time of trouble. God's will was to allow a little hardship for a greater glorification of His name. Certainly the results were beyond spectacular as Jesus raised Lazarus from the dead, however had he not adhered to the will of God the results very possibly would not have occurred at all. As Christians, the capability of hearing and understanding the will of God is nothing in comparison to that of Jesus Christ. At times, hearing anything from God *at all* seems an impossible task. Even so, there is a way to hear it in the case of healing.

The Gift of Healing will be discussed in detail in a later chapter. However, for those who have that gift there is a simple exercise to discover the will of God in individual circumstances. Throughout the gospels, particularly in Matthew and in Mark, Jesus exposed a precursor to the act of healing. That precursor was compassion. In Matthew 14:14 Jesus healed the sick because He was "moved with compassion." Because of compassion He multiplied the fish to feed the multitudes in Matthew 15. In Matthew 20 He healed the blind because of compassion. In Mark 1 He cleansed the leaper because of compassion. Throughout the Bible it is compassion that drives Christ to heal. Because Jesus only did the will of the Father, compassion *must* have been the Father's will for those situations. As Christians begin to explore the gift of healing and praying for the sick it is imperative to listen and look for compassion. It is easy to have compassion for a loved one, but remember, the place Christ could heal only a few was His own hometown (Matthew 13: 57-58). In fact, while in his hometown of Nazareth, Jesus said, *"A prophet is not without honor except in his home town, and in his own household. And He did not do many miracles..."* It is compassion felt for a stranger that is an even stronger indication of God's will, and a sign to a believer that God wants to act in the instance. The correct response to this seemingly misplaced compassion is to pray for the object of that compassion. This could be for healing, or any other need, but the compassion is the key. Compassion for a perfect stranger is a practical example of God revealing His will to the believer.

Even though the experience of godly compassion is a powerful practical example of God's will being revealed, it is in no way a guarantee that the believer is perfectly lined up with the will of

7

God. Compassion is a human emotion and it is possible, particularly with loved ones, that its' presence is purely human. Though misplaced compassion with a stranger is a good indication of the will of God, with loved ones compassion may simply be innate, and not according to God's will. Jesus knew this with Lazarus. He had compassion, but in this instance He relied on the Holy Spirit to overrule that compassion. Jesus knew through the Holy Spirit that the correct thing to do was to tarry two days before going to Lazarus. This was contrary to His desire to go immediately because He loved him. The Father had a specific act of faith in the case of Lazarus that overruled the compassion. The Father's will was not expressed in the generic form of compassion, but rather had a specific act of faith included with its expression. There are numerous incidents of healing both in the bible and throughout history where the will of God was very specific, or required a specific act of faith. A classic example from Christ's life comes in the healing of a blind man.

This particular account occurs in John 9: 1-7. The healing concluded in verse 6 & 7 as the reader discovers Jesus, *"spat on the ground, and made clay of the spittle, and applied the clay to his eyes... and he came back seeing."* Christ did nothing that did not come from the Father, and incredibly discerned that God wanted clay made from spit in order to accomplish the healing in this man. Frankly it is a disgusting thought, yet a dramatic reminder that God's wisdom can appear foolish, as was said in 1 Corinthians 1:21. *"God was well-pleased through the foolishness of the message preached to save those who believe."* Here God saved a man's eye sight, along with his soul. Time and time again the healing of the Bible was not a generic laying on of hands or generic adherence to the broad will of God. Jesus told lepers on one occasion to wash themselves, and on another to show themselves to the priest. For the Roman Centurion's servant He simply gave the word that he was healed. Sometimes Christ spoke a word, other times he delivered healing with a touch. With every variation there was a specific will of God communicated to Christ through the Holy Spirit.

For me personally, many times, I have prayed for the sick & dying with very specific instructions from the Holy Spirit. I will limit myself to one example so as to not contaminate any instructions the reader may hear as they pray. But this account took place in Ciudad de Victoria, Mexico.

As part of Ministry School the members of my class were required to go on a mission trip to Ciudad de Victoria. It was a wonderful trip, filled with learning and experiencing an incredible display by God for both salvations and healing. On the last day of the trip our group decided to forego sight seeing and shopping to instead go into the local dump and minister to some people who found the location suitable to squatting and a place to forage for food. There in the stench and squalor we sent up a medical tent to dispense common over the counter medication and even had a licensed Mexican physician to give medical exams. Each person was given the opportunity to see the doctor, and each person was given a portion of beans, rice, four, and oil. I would have to say that 100% of the people took advantage of all that we had brought and the line that formed to enter the medical tent was quite long.

Prior to arrival at the tent, my fellow ministry students and I all had the opportunity to pray for the people entering. Upon exit, the residents were once again prayed for. Most of these people were elderly women. If I were to guess, I would say the average age approached 60. Another unusual fact was that many appeared to have cataracts in various forms and stages. Believing God heals and having never seen the blind receive sight, I was all too engaged in exploring prayer and testing, to a degree, what God was going to do with this downtrodden, outcast segment of this society. Stationed outside the medical tent with 2 other ministers we would have the patients sit in a folding chair so that we could lay our hands upon them and pray. Many immediately felt healings from their common ailments. Emerging from the tent lead by another much younger woman came a grey haired, feeble in posture, senior citizen. As she sat in the now infamous chair it was clear to see that she was completely blinded by cataracts. Pouncing like a cat on a mouse, three young ministers descended with outstretched hands and prayers to beg God's healing hand to touch this woman. As we prayed it appeared as if nothing was going to happen. So I stopped praying for the woman and began asking God, what do we do? In that instance the Holy Spirit said, **"see with my eyes, not with yours."** Stopping the prayers I lifted my hands from the woman and searched the depths of my mind and soul, desperate to see with God's eyes. In an instant I saw a vision of the three of us praying for the woman. The difference in the vision and reality was a simple positioning of my hands. What I saw was my left hand was on top of the woman's head and my right hand on the back of her head. So obeying this instruction of this vision I laid my hands as I had seen them. Instantaneously the woman jumped from her seat and shouted in Spanish, "I can see." Looking at one another in astonishment we said, "You can?" For me that was the beginning of trying to discover the exact prescribed will of God in individual healing. I have seen God heal hundreds of people, but when asked how, I always reply, "it has nothing to do with me,

I just try to get in God's way." In finding the perfect will of God and stepping out in faith on what that will is believed to be, the miracle can be witnessed. If the Christian can first discover the will of God in a matter of healing, then when the actual prayer is prayed it is simply getting in the way of what God already was intent on doing. To the minister that prays for healing, the miracle itself is independent of the individual. Rather, it is what God has chosen for that moment to make the very same minister a witness. Experience in hundreds of hospital bedside visits dictates that the greatest question of God that can be asked is, "What are You going to do Lord?" My experiences of seeing the lame walk, the blind see, and even the dead raised are not because of any special gift within me, but rather an ability to sometimes perceive what the will of God is and to jump in the middle of it.

Carlos Anacondia wrote that he visited insane asylums for the exposure to demonically oppressed and possessed people. There he witnessed God setting free perhaps thousands of people. But the point of his frequent visits was to place himself in a target rich environment. For this author, the years of hospital visitations were for the very same reason; to be in a target rich environment and give God the maximum opportunity to heal and be a witness thereof. Yet in so many cases there were times when the results were not what I expected or desired. The healing was not to my order. Given enough opportunity the healing power of God will be witnessed, and the conflict of human agenda versus God's agenda will also be encountered. The compassion felt cannot overcome the will of God or destiny of the individual. In those times it becomes imperative to return to the written will of God. It is imperative to understand what Christ said in Matthew 25:36, *"I was sick, and you visited Me..."* There are times when *that* is what going to the sick is about... *visiting.* The Bible is written with purpose and the more it is understood the less fallible it becomes. Jesus did not say, I was sick and you healed Me, or I was sick and you prayed for me. No, the command is "visit." In the words of a great southerner... everything else is gravy. It is the command to visit and its pertinence to the will of God that leads to the exploration of the sovereign will of God.

Beyond this individually prescribed will that God has for individual lives, there is the sovereign will of God. God in being sovereign possesses supreme authority. He can act with or without cause. He can cause a healing in the complete absence of any of the remaining four aspects being discussed here. There can be times when the individual will of God is for a person's healing and any of the remaining four aspects prevent it. Yet there is never an instance when God, in his sovereignty, decides to heal that something or someone can prevent it. A prime example of this is found in John 5 2-7. There Jesus encounters a man who had been sick for thirty-eight years. The Bible explains that from time to time an angel would come and stir the pool by the Sheep's gate, and that the first one to enter would be healed. Jesus asks this man (who had many times lost the race to the pool by those less afflicted) if he would like to be made well. The man does not say, yes. Instead he chose to explain how he is never fast enough to the pool first. Without approval, without a request, without any acknowledgment or prompting of Christ by the man, Jesus made him well when He said, **"Arise, take up your pallet, and walk."** Sovereignly, God healed though Christ. But that was 2000 years ago--what is God doing today? He is doing **the very same thing**.

Several years back, the church I was attending decided to host a large Thanksgiving dinner. Invited to the event were the poor of the neighborhood and other underprivileged groups. Included in this group were some geriatric patients at a local rest home. I call them "old folks." My volunteer assignment at the time was to pray for the table of old folks.

Perhaps some of you take offense at the term old folks. But that is what I called them. To me, they had lived their life and there was nothing appealing about them to me spiritually, emotionally, or otherwise. In fact, my heart was in such poor condition, I would go so far as to say I had genuine distaste for the elderly, and my terminology was a simple manifestation of what was in my heart. However, God, in His infinite wisdom, was about to begin the long process of breaking that attitude and reshaping my heart. My assignment met with complete disdain, and I certainly had no expectations of miraculous results as I prayed for the people at this table.

So I walked to the table, putting on a plastic smile and equally disingenuous attitude, and started at one end of the table and prayed for those who asked as I went. I don't know how many people were there at the table, but it had to be at least 50. As I came down the first side, about the middle of the table I looked at a couple just immediately across the table when the Holy Spirit spoke. He said, "I am going to heal both of them, pray for his wife first." To me this was no big deal; I have heard God express His will many times. What it did mean is that, given the direction I was headed, I would have to skip the man to pray for his wife first. Upon making my way to the couple I noticed the gentleman had a four-post walker. I had not seen him come in, and did not know his condition, but I was confident God would heal him, so I proclaimed to him, "God is going to heal you."

His response… "Don't you bullshit me boy."

Sorry, but that's what he said… and in **church** at that! So I said, "I don't care what you say. God told me he was going to heal you and to prove it; He is going to heal your wife first."

He obviously didn't believe me, or even seem to care, but without further hesitation I proceeded to pray for his wife, and as expected God immediately healed her. It was so insignificant I cannot even remember her troubles. But this cranky old goat was a whole other story. He had a host of ailments and was barely able to walk. I began to pray. Memory fades a bit at this point, but again it has never been about me. It is about God, so whatever I do or say pales in comparison to the Lord God coming to earth and moving. I do remember putting both hands on his knees, and when I was done I asked him how he felt. Again, my questioning met with the same tart response. So I told him. "Rise and walk in the name of Jesus." Working his way to his feet ever so gently, he began to stand as if nothing had changed. Suddenly he was hit with an epiphany that his pains weren't what they were moments earlier. The cautious moved changed to deliberate. The deliberate moves changed to celebratory. Then, without notice, the four post walker was snatched into the sky, and the brazen, cranky old goat has suddenly changed in body and personality. Gone was the profanity, replaced by shouting of "God healed me… I can walk!" With a walker in one hand, raised high overhead, he continued the chant and celebration of God all the way to the bus that brought him. God, in a sovereign act, healed that man completely. The healing was not because I am a pious man, but rather was a lesson to me that God's love and desires to heal are not bound by age. Even though I prayed completely against my will, God wanted to show me His love. Likewise it had nothing to do with that man's attitude, because it was less than receptive. It was God doing what He wanted to do when He wanted to do it. But such is not the case in every instance. There remain four other factors at work in every healing. All or which are completely supported by the word of God. As will be discovered, it can never be said that God contradicts Himself or is inconsistent. That is a human trait. Rather God is consistently pursuing relationship with His people and will sacrifice everything to make relationship a reality.

FAITH OF THE RECEIVER

I ncluded in the five factors that must be explored to understand the inconsistency of healing is faith. This notion of faith
dominates the New Testament, after barely an appearance
in the Old Testament. In places it is used as an adjective. to describe
a person's character, and in others used as a noun to represent some
mystical power. But what is it? Only a little will move mountains according to Jesus, but yet so many people lack it. By faith the Christian
is saved. By faith people are healed. Hebrews 11:1 defines faith as *"the
assurance of things hoped for, the conviction of things not seen."*
However, this definition does little to clarify this ambiguous term. It
does say that faith is not hope but rather assurance. It does not define faith on the basis of results, in that it is the conviction of unseen
results. Ministers have asked congregations to stir up their faith, but
without understanding what it is, how can it be stirred.

Paul told the Romans in 10:17, *"Faith comes from hearing, and hearing by the word of Christ."* Will simple reading the gospels create faith? Will hearing sermon after sermon produce faith? Perhaps, or perhaps not. Faith is one of those godly traits that seem to be present or not. Some even have more than others, as Abraham was the Father of Faith. If deductive reasoning is used to describe the invisible, mysterious notion of faith, then perhaps when a Christian hears from God, accompanied in that voice is an assurance, a certainty that the object of faith will be accomplished. Faith perhaps is best described as a trust in God. Said yet another way, perhaps faith is simply the opposite or even absence of doubt.

In Matthew 14 the story of Peter walking on the water is told. As he was walking, Peter was being distracted by the wind and waves, and began to sink. In verse 31 Jesus asks him, *"why did you doubt?"* In Matthew 21:21 Jesus says that *"if you have faith and do not doubt"* you can move mountains. Therefore doubt, or the lack of it, is as important an ingredient in God moving as this notion of faith. For that reason the definition to be used for this discussion of faith is the absence of doubt. Certainly, if God were to speak in an audible voice commanding a prayer for healing, no doubt would be present. So too a word spoken by the Holy Spirit in the silence of the soul can dispel this same doubt and conversely produce faith. But to hear the voice of God, to not doubt necessitates a subjective relationship with God far beyond the objective knowing of Him.

To continue with this line of reasoning, doubt is formed out of a lack of relationship. Non-Christians doubt salvation through Christ because they have never experienced Him and doubt His existence. Husbands and wives doubt their spouses when over time trust is broken. Parents doubt their children when the evidence indicates something to the contrary. So too, a lack in a relationship to God brings faith-killing doubt. For that matter, being unrepentant in your sin can also often bring doubt. It is in the fullness of God's forgiveness that His love is felt and that doubt disappears. It is in that intimacy with God that super-human faith is established. This in no way suggests that a person receiving prayer for healing must have a relationship with Christ. It simply suggests that it is imperative for the person praying to have that relationship. What is important to understand is this paradigm with relationship to God and faith. Without digressing to a related theological discussion it must be understood that God's entire purpose with human kind is to create relationship with Him. Nothing pleases Him more. It is the purpose of heaven, to be with Him. It was the purpose of Christ dying, to permanently restore the ability to have a relationship with the Father as Adam & Eve had enjoyed. With that in mind, every miracle of God is there for the very same purpose. To create, reestablish, or promote an individual's relationship to Him. There have been many miracles upon the unsaved that led to salvation, just as there have been many that were witnessed and brought relationship to an audience or neighbor. Ultimately, the person receiving the prayer will understand this aspect. As said before, a very small minority are concerned about anything other than their relationship to God on their death bed.

For the saved person, faith in their possession can heal them. No better place is this displayed than in the miracles of Matthew 9. Here is the story of the woman with the issue of blood. By Jewish law this woman should not have been in public as she was considered unclean. And yet she fights through a crowd to simply touch Jesus. She had no doubt in her mind that if she could just touch Him that she would be healed. And this is exactly what occurred. Jesus says in verse 22 ***"Daughter, take courage; your faith has made you well."*** It was her faith that caused the miracle. Her lack of doubt touched the Father and through Christ she received a healing. Her faith led her to go in public and fight through hundreds, perhaps thousands of people to get to Jesus. Her faith cast the law and man's opinions aside to go after her healing. Had she not made it to Jesus, or had her faith not brought her to healing, then the crowd could have legally stoned her to death as being in public and touching others in her unclean state was a capital offense.

Later in the same chapter Jesus encounters two blind men. When He heals them His statement is *"Be it done according to your faith."* He did not say be it done according to *my* faith. On the contrary, He makes a point for all of history that their faith was at the very root of the miracle being a success. The absence of doubt restored sight to these blind men. What is particularly interesting about this expression of faith is that these two men lack the normal human faculties to even make a reasonable assumption as to the person of Jesus. They couldn't see Him, but had only heard. They certainly had no visual proof of any of the claims. They were simply wandering through the street crying out to him because they heard the word of God. In hearing their faith was created.

Further evidence of the importance of the faith of the receiver is shown in numerous accounts where the lack of faith *prevented* miracles. More often than not a person will look at humanity rather than God as their source of faith. People tend to base their faith on the person praying instead of God. Jesus was a prime example of this in our earlier account where He could perform few miracles in His hometown. Why? There were few miracles, healing or otherwise, because they saw Him as the son of a carpenter, not the Son of God. So too goes the world today. Someone in need of God's healing bases their faith in the person who prays rather than their faith in God Himself. Perhaps they can't believe if an unknown shows up at their bedside, because they wanted their pastor to be there.

While in Argentina I met a man by the name of Pastor Benedito. He is known all over South America and pastors a church of several thousand. The man is humble in stature, and when I met him for the first time at the airport in Cordoba, Argentina I thought he was the gardener. In fact, my Spanish was so bad it was hours later that I discovered our driver was not the gardener, but in fact the Pastor we had come to see. In three days this humble man, who I did not know from Adam, would teach me more about healing than three thousand sermons had done before him, and than a thousand sermons have since. By American standards this man would not fill a bus with parishioners, let alone a stadium, as is common today for some. Yet from the comfort of his less than two thousand square foot home he answered my questions and those of my fellow ministers for hours upon hours. At the end of the trip he prayed for us all, and all of us received healing. For me, I received healing for a ruptured disc in my neck, documented with before and after x-rays. The biggest lesson of that trip to Argentina was not my own healing. It was the lesson that God often hides treasures in people that offend us. Get past the offense, and you will receive the key that will unlock that treasure. God will serve the prideful through the humble and healing can come in any vessel.

God moves independent of the vessel. The person praying is a vessel and it does not matter if they are a champagne glass or a Dixie cup. To doubt that God would use the least of us is to doubt in God's ability to heal. Need we be reminded of Balaam's donkey and how God used an ass to talk to a prophet? To be in the proper place to receive healing the infirmed must focus on God, and not doubt God's ability. Man will **always** fail, and apart from God there is no ability to heal. Unless of course modern medicine, in all it's imperfection, is counted as healing.

Solomon in his wisdom wrote in Ecclesiastes 1:9, *"...nothing is new under the sun,"* and this is still true today. Though information has increased, man's capacity to process that information has not. Though personality and human frailties have been defined and documented to a greater extent, there is nothing new about the human psyche today from 2000 years ago. As such, the flaws revealed about human kind in the Bible are true today as well. Five times in the gospels Jesus pointed out that His disciples were of "little faith." The very hand chosen men of God who were to carry on the first message of Christ were people of little faith. How much more then can the common man of today can be described as such? When eyes are focused on the vessel, then doubt is the absolute end result. For the people of Nazareth, their focus was on anything but the Savior. Their own questions in Matthew 13:53-58 reveal this doubt when they ask, *"Where did this man get this wisdom, and these miraculous powers? Is not this the carpenter's son? Is not His mother called Mary..."* The people of Nazareth were focused on the package and not the present inside. This doubt according to scripture was the reason "He did not do many miracles there because of their unbelief."

There are many cases of unbelief, doubt, and lack of faith in the New Testament, yet this remains the only example where miracles were stopped because of it. Yet in churches, hospitals, and homes, this least of the influences of not receiving a healing miracle remains the most blamed. Could it not possibly be God prohibiting it? Could it not possibly be the faith of the minister? It must be the faith of the person praying. Nothing could be further than the truth. Yes, faith of the receiver is important, but if it were an absolute must then the unsaved would never receive a healing. Contrary to common thought, it can be argued that the faith of the person praying is equally important. For certain, in every instance of healing portrayed in the Bible there was faith in the equation. When the audience had little faith, Christ's faith was enough. When the audience did have faith, it was universally applauded by Jesus Himself. The point is that if a miracle of healing doesn't happen at the hands of the most world renowned television evangelists, do not make the assumption it was a lack of faith on the recipients. Simply understand that faith is one of five components.

Jesus had absolute faith. And only once, in His hometown of Nazareth does the Bible say He was reduced in His capacity to perform miracles. God is not limited, but as will be discovered, He will limit His displays based on the character of the parties involved.

FAITH OF THE PRAYER

D
oubt is a very evil thing. It is a key instrument in preventing a relationship with God. Not doubt in the form of not believing the existence of God, but rather doubt in ourselves. Christians for centuries now have walked in a sense of condemnation. Afraid to approach the Father in prayer, even though Paul so pointedly informs us in Romans 8:1 *"... there is no condemnation in Christ."* In order to overcome doubt in ourselves, we must come to understanding of the love of God. Christians must embrace the very notion that they can approach God not because of their own acts of righteousness but because Christ made appropriation for all sin, past, present and future. Therefore knowing everyone has sinned, is sinning, and will sin again, the words of Hebrews 4:16 must be acted upon when it says, *"Therefore let us draw near with confidence to the throne of*

grace, so that we may receive mercy and find grace to help in time of need." It is imperative to lay aside the self-doubt that God will use the common for the uncommon miracle, and instead approach Him with all confidence knowing He has grace and mercy for a time of need. Eliminate doubt from the thought process, draw near in confidence. Not because it is deserved, but draw near knowing it was Christ very purpose and God's ultimate desire.

There are a thousand secular materials available that encourage and claim power in positive thinking. Their underlying commonality is that if a person makes a positive declaration enough then they will become that declaration. Believe what you want about this, but it certainly contains some applicable truth here. If doubt is an issue, then the proper thing to do is to dwell on the positive truth. Paul to the Philippians wrote in 4:8, *"...whatever is true, whatever is honorable, whatever is right, whatever is pure, whatever is lovely, whatever is of good repute, if there is any excellence and if anything worthy of praise, dwell on these things."* Paul was giving the motivational speech of his time. He was saying, stop dwelling on the bad, stop allowing doubt to be your focus, but rather if there is the smallest shred of good in you, dwell on that. In accomplishing this exercise the Christian can begin the process of removing doubt, building confidence not for the purpose of healing someone, but to approach the throne of God. By finding the good in oneself, the image that God has of us emerges. As that picture emerges then the relationship is fostered. Out of the relationship miracles will occur.

Faith (the absence of doubt) heals. More than once a crowd brings Jesus a lame man that God healed because as Jesus put it, "their faith." Their faith was the primary fuel supply for the miracle. In Luke, 7:9 Jesus says of a Centurion Soldier, *"...not even in Israel have I found such great faith."* Here a Roman soldier, a non-Jew, approached Christ to say, *"...just say the word and my servant will be healed."* And the servant was healed without a visit of touch from Jesus, merely on the faith of the Centurion. Faith of a mustard seed says to the mountain to fall into the sea and it happens. Faith of less than a mustard seed says to the mountain, fall into the sea, then goes to a hardware store for a shovel to make it happen. In Mark 2 is just a story of such faith. *"And they came bringing to Him a paralytic, carried by four men. And being unable to get to Him because of the crowd, they removed the roof above Him; and when they had dug an opening, they let down the pallet on which the paralytic was lying."* Christ saw their faith through effort and healed the lame man. These four men did not tear the roof off just any house. According to verse 1 they tore the roof off Jesus' personal home. Bold faith sent them in confidence to the throne where they found mercy and grace. God is looking for such boldness in all of Christianity to approach Him. Doubt must be dealt with to approach God, but once there, all remaining doubt will disappear. James wrote in Chapter 2: 18, *"You have faith and I have works; show me faith without works and I will show you my faith by my works."* Faith has a corresponding action, and action at the command of God produces faith. The lame man's friends manifested their faith with their actions. They knew Jesus could heal and they did everything humanly possible to get their friend to Him, including tearing the roof off His house. The woman with the issue of blood ventured into public, waded through the crowd, and with a certain death sentence for her actions went until she found Jesus. Their faith was demonstrated in their actions because they had no doubt He would heal them. Anyone can put a hand on a forehead and pray in a crowd of Christians. God is bigger than this, and He is looking for those without doubt or shame.

It could be argued that for a miracle to occur some portion faith must be present, either in the recipient or in the vessel. Faith moves God's heart, not magic words or a human touch. As in the story of the Centurion, Jesus was not in the same local, and faith brought the servants healing. Jesus did not touch the Lepers when He healed them, but instead in one instance commanded them to go and show themselves to the Chief Priest. Watch a Benny Hinn crusade and one can witness people being healed by God without even a specific prayer going up. They come to the stage and testify of what God had done in them while at the service. Their healing occurred before coming to the stage. It is not Benny Hinn, it is God. I am sure Benny has developed incredible faith over the years, but these people come with an expectation and confidence God will touch them there, and it is their faith that will often be the necessary fuel and motivation for God to act.

Faith in the form of the absence of doubt is very powerful. And yet doubt remains one of those many things that are uniquely human. There is not one instance where science has ever measured doubt in an animal. A dog does not doubt his master will feed him. A bird does not doubt it can fly (well, perhaps that *is* the ostrich's problem). In fact science says a bubble bee should be unable to fly, and without a doubt it does. Jesus said in Matthew 6:26, ***"Look at the birds of the air, that they do not sow, nor reap, nor gather into barns, and yet your heavenly Father feeds them. Are you not worth much more than they?"*** Contextually, He was discussing anxiety. Anxiety is a symptom of doubt. Doubt, if you will, is the cause of the symptom. Letting go of this uniquely human trait by trusting in God enables Him to work in the lives of mankind.

God is infinite and infinitely capable of doing anything at anytime. One evangelist of old was known for punching people in the stomach and God healing them. Carlos Anacondia in South America has seen thousands of healing and demonic deliverances. He is known of turning the sound system up so loud in his service your ears will nearly bleed. He does so because of a scripture that says to shout the word of God. But punching people, turning up microphones, pushing them over with a hand on the forehead is not what heals. It is God that heals. The point is, man tries to find patterns that work. Man tries to find a formula that produces consistent results, but God is not limited to formulas. If rolling in cow dung is what He wants to cure a person then it will. The question is will the person praying believe the command that heals or will they doubt? Conversely, just because Jesus spit in the dirt, made clay and healed a blind man, there is absolutely no assurance that will ever work again. What works is faith.

It is important to not confuse style with God. As humans we create a style. Our style of prayer, dress, or performance will not interfere with God's ability . In fact, God may even prescribe a style to you for your own sake and for convenience. I say this because over time I have come to my own God-prescribed style when ministering to the sick. In the course of my life I have two different types of events in which I pray for the sick. One type is in the course of a service when I am invited to pray as a lay minister. Secondly, is in a visitation of some sort like a hospital. There is no particular service or style of praying that I subscribe to. However with the visitations, I have a much more prescribed pattern, if you will. Assuming the person is conscious, speaks English, and is not a child, I will first do what I call a salvation check. Remember Jesus said, "I was sick and you visited me." I go with the intent of a visit. I inquire about their conditions, and with the innocence of a dove probe their relationship with Christ. If unsaved, I proceed to talk about Christ. If saved, I move on to building their faith through first hand testimonies of God's grace and healing abilities. I consciously sow seeds of faith into them. At the same time my own faith increases, as I remind myself of the things God has done before. The Bible says to "encourage one another," and this pattern of visiting and encouraging are all intent on helping that person's relationship to Christ, and with the hope of witnessing a miracle. Many times the miracle is witnessed, and many times it is not. It is not because God can be fooled or tricked into acting. He knows what is in the absolute best interest of us all even when the life it creates is less than pleasurable. God is at work to conform us to Christ and if that means 40 days in the desert, tossed by waves in storm, or bearing a cross, He will allow it. For the Christian, the primary concern has got to be where does our individual relationship stand with Him? When a miracle occurs, rejoice with those who rejoice. When it does not, head to an alone time with God and search your heart and His as to why it didn't happen. Go in confidence and without doubt to God, and ask if your faith failed. Even in God's will and full of faith, miracles can still remain absent. When this happens, perhaps the consistency of the inconsistency is found with the motives of the heart.

MOTIVES

James 4:3 states, *"You ask and do not receive, because y*
ask with the wrong motives, so that you may spend it (
your pleasures." There is no more difficult a lesson for
Christian to learn than when a prayer that has gone unanswere
because of wrong motives. Equally there is no more difficult
task than to search within ourselves to find the truth of our own
motivation. Faith enough to fill a dump truck and absolute approval of God will not overcome selfish motives when it comes to
experiencing His miracles of healing. Selfish motives and God's
miracles are as incompatible as oil and water. James mentions
lustful motives when he describes spending on your pleasures, and
lust for financial benefit will certainly squelch the power of God to
heal. Equally debilitating are motives related to pride. Ministers
whose believe in their hearts that healing will bring their ministry

notoriety or fame are highly unlikely to experience the healing miracles of God.

My first experience of the incompatibility of pride and God's power came during my second mission trip to Mexico. In the weeks leading up to this mission trip I was in prayer daily and fasting every other day. In my heart I felt that if God is going to use me as a minister, then I want to be the best minister I can be. Like a fighter who prepares for a title bout, I prepared spiritually as best I knew how, expecting God to do big things in the heart of the people I would encounter. With this state of mind in consideration, the night before leaving I had a dream. In that dream I saw myself preaching my message in a small church. In this small church was a chair on the front row, just to my right, that was different from all the other seating. Seated in that chair was an elderly woman, dressed in a blue flower print sundress. Her hair was completely grey and she was completely blind. The dream began towards the end of my message and as I concluded my message I saw myself taking some water from the illustration to my sermon and putting it on the woman's eyes. I woke to the shock of her receiving sight. I knew with all my being this was a prophetic dream.

Days later we arrived at the small community church where I was to preach. As I walked through the door for the first time, my

heart raced as it appeared to be the exact place in my dream. As the service began I noticed the chair. It was a white plastic chair similar to one you might buy at Sam's or some other discount outlet. The rest of the seating could be described as hand crafted wood benches. Actually more like boards on some milk cartons, but you get the picture. My eyes were glued to that chair. As the service started with worship that chair remained empty. About three quarters of the way through worship my continuous peeking revealed what God has shown me nights earlier. Escorted by the arm of one of the other church women, a grey haired elderly woman came into the church. Hair pulled tight in a nice bun, just as I had seen in the dream. Dressed in the baby blue sundress as well. I thought to myself, could this be the woman? She was led to that one white plastic chair.

Curiosity is not something that festers in me long. I immediate left my place to ask the woman escorting her in if the little old lady was blind. She told me that she was. An explosion of faith took place in me. My heart raced, my body shook. In confidence, at the beginning of the service I called the woman out and told her, and the congregation, that God was going to heal her. I was so excited to see the blind receive sight for the first time that I rushed through my sermon and grabbed the vase of water used for my illustration and went immediately to the woman upon completion. Interpreter in tow, I asked if I could put some of the water on her eyes. She agreed and I prayed for God to restore her sight. Expecting a miracle, I asked through the interpreter if she could see. She said, "My eyes hurt when I came in, but they don't hurt any more." So I explained to her that even Jesus had to pray more than once for a blind person and consequently grabbed twice as much water for round two. Again I asked, "Can you see?" Her reply was "I can see a little light, but I still can't see." Again and again I prayed for her. Every other minister prayed for her, but the end results were no better than a little light.

I was heartbroken. How could God take me so far and not do His part? Crying I got on the bus that had brought us there. My fellow ministers trying to comfort me, but I was having none of it. I went straight to my bed as soon as we arrived at the mission. Sobbing on my bed I asked God, "why?" It was then I heard, "Because of your pride you did not see that woman receive her sight." Tears of heartbreak and disappointment turned to tears of repentance. In that instant my heart was shown to me, and it was ugly. Instantly I knew my ultimate motivation was to outshine the other ministers. In that instance the jealousy of others having bigger audiences or better services was revealed.

So I asked the Lord again, what must I do? To that the Holy Spirit reminded me of James 5:16, *"Therefore, confess your sins to one another, and pray for one another so that you may be healed. The effective prayer of a righteous man can accomplish much."* I knew what I had to do. To remove the prideful motive I had to confess it. So I went, first to a man by the name of Mark Baker and told him how I was jealous of the favor he received. To that, and to my surprise, he confessed to me things he held against me. This spread through the ministers like wildfire and in the coming days we all witnessed incredible healing miracles of God.

Anything other than humble motives will cause what God is doing to be missed. God did not say because of pride the woman was not healed. God said because of pride I did not get to see it. I was completely unaware on any conscious level that I had a pride issue. It was there and it was God's judgment through the Holy Spirit that revealed it. As Christians who are forbidden to judge one another, it is critical to have a relationship with God so that there can be moments together where He can not only judge our heart and motives, but also provide the surgery to repair them. It is in this relationship of allowing the Holy Spirit to judge us that keeps us from the motives of the Scribes and Pharisees where Jesus quoted Isaiah in Matthew 15:8, *"This people honors Me with this lips, but their heart is far away from me."*

If healing is prayed for and healing does not occur, the first act for all parties should be to get before God and probe deep into their hearts. There should not be a discussion or theological debate but time spent alone and individually approaching God. God forbid that Christ should have to repeat the Isaiah scripture found in Matthew 13:15, *"For the heart of this people has become dull, and with their ears they scarcely hear, and they have closed their eyes, otherwise they would see with their eyes, hear with their ears, and understand with their heart and return, and I would heal them."* The prophet was speaking metaphorically about the eyes and ears of the heart. Motives of the heart cannot be addressed by the Holy Spirit when the heart is dull and unwilling to listen or see the truth about itself. Forsaking those motives and returning to God brings healing according to scripture. Matthew 13 – 15 is rich with discussion about the heart. And the motives of the heart are what defile man and prevent God from moving. Jesus said in Matthew 15:18, *"But the things that proceed out of the mouth come from the heart, and those defile the man."* Nothing had come from my mouth in the weeks preceding the encounter with the blind woman other than prayers. Literally nothing had gone in my mouth as I had fasted for days before and yet my prideful heart defiled me and prevented the witness of God's act.

Is it possible to be truly and wholly concerned for the sick, independent of ulterior motives? Is it possible to see an audience of tens of thousands flocking to a minister used by God to heal and not be jealous of the hundreds of thousands of dollars each night those services bring into the ministry? Is anyone uncontaminated by greed, lust, or pride? If there *were* such a person the world would not have needed Christ. But when these emotional sins are confessed, as James proclaims the power is stolen and humility takes their place. God cannot be fooled. He knows what is in the heart of the unbeliever and believer alike. The greatest deception that hinders God's power does not occur when the world perceives something other than what is truly in the individual. The greatest deception occurs when the Christian does not recognize and acknowledge the flaws within himself. Overcoming the frailty will hopefully occur in time. The acknowledgment of the frailty is more important to God than overcoming it. Even when one frailty is admitted and overcome, it is inevitable that another, less visible one will become the focus of God's transformation.

The Bible says healing will follow those who believe, and in such, all of Christianity should be praying for the healing of others.

For the lay person, falling into the lustful side of pride is not likely to be common. However, the fearful side of pride is quite common in the laity. In the average Christian there is another aspect of pride that prevents God's power from moving as well. For the average Christian, praying for the sick is embarrassing. To act out in faith on an unspoken word of God calling for action can be equally embarrassing. It is this embarrassment that points to wrong motives. Embarrassment says the opinion of someone as a reflection of us is more important than the love God wants to express to the individual in need. Embarrassment can be fear of ridicule or it could actually be a self devaluation. In the presence of members who they perceive to be spiritually superior, the Christian will forgo praying for someone for fear of embarrassing themselves. No matter how hard the Holy Spirit tugs on the heart, fear of embarrassment can prevent the inner call to pray. Embarrassment is an indication that motives need to be checked. It is a good indicator that the love of God and the love of others is not the priority.

God is not inconsistent. But God is incomprehensible. The basics are certainly comprehensible. The fact that God is love can be understood to a degree, but when one dives into it they find it to be a vast and bottomless abyss. Yet at the very surface of that love is the desire to have a relationship with mankind. Each layer of understanding is followed by a question of uncertainty related to this seeming inconsistency. The questioning created by the seeming inconsistency is all designed to draw the Christian closer and closer to God. The obvious affect of healing on an unsaved person is that God is real, and that God is love. The obscure is when the prayer goes unanswered or the healing does not occur. God is not inconsistent, but rather consistently drawing us to Him. He is consistent about having mankind come to Him for answers so that He can reveal Himself. The king does not go to the peasant. The peasant comes to the King. God is consistently sending messages through unanswered prayer for the believer to come to Him, and in coming to Him the believer's heart is judged. The dross within is consistently revealed, and hopefully removed.

Hebrews 9:27 says, ***"And inasmuch as it is appointed for men to die once and after this comes judgment."*** Everyone dies, and the timing of it is of little or no consequence to God. What is important is the judgment that follows. The undeniable miraculous affect of healing, or lack thereof, is an incredible tool for God to judge the hearts of man here on earth, so that they will not be judged later. Healing is a tool, nothing more, nothing less, for God to build relationship. That relationship can increase equally whether or not the healing actually occurs. If motives are changed for the better because God forgoes His touch, then so be it. If a life comes to salvation because a healing occurs then so be it. God knows the end of the beginning according to Isaiah. Isaiah 46:10, ***"Declaring the end from the beginning, and from ancient times things which have not been done, saying, 'My purpose will be established, and I will accomplish all My good pleasure.'"*** Healing as a tool accomplishes God's good pleasure of relationship, the beginning of which is painfully obvious, the end of which is known only to Him.

I am reminded of a visit to Methodist Hospital in Houston. I was called by a friend to come and pray for a young mother who was in NICU for a brain aneurism. All prognoses were bad, and the doctors did not expect this woman to recover. Arriving at the hospital, my friend introduced me to the family in the waiting room. Not just a mother and father, but the whole family. Included in the number were her husband, children, mother, father, siblings, and a host of people. This group of people complicated the entire process, because in order to pray for someone in ICU, I first needed permission of the family. The problem was that they were all unsaved, and to describe their lack of faith as simply disbelief would be kind. So asking their permission to pray for their loved one was not well received, and ended up turning to a theological discussion. All the wisdom in me and the help of the Holy Spirit seemed to be of no avail. They were not convinced salvation was the path for them, and moreover, they were angry at God that such a fate had befallen a wife and daughter. I was embarrassed to even ask them to pray for their loved one. If I couldn't convince them God was real, then how could I convince them to let me walk in faith for her healing. In the end they allowed me to pray anyway. In boldness I asked them to allow God to prove himself, to which they agreed.

The ICU was very busy. My friend also wanted to pray with me and in the chaos I can't tell you a word of what was said or done. What I can tell you is that immediately the young lady began to recover. Her recovery was so miraculous that the entire family ended up committing their lives to Christ. No longer was I ministering to them, but in a few short days they were the ones proclaiming God's goodness to me, something that would be much needed in the days to come.

The ICU is a very bad place. Even with all the care taken by those fine physicians and nurses, it remains a hotbed for other diseases, as was the case with this woman. As she recovered from the aneurism she was stricken with a disease called ARDS, or Adult Respiratory Distress Syndrome. It is a super bug related to pneumonia. As fast as this woman's brain was healing, to the point she could sit up and talk, a disease was destroying her lungs. Of course we prayed, trusting God would continue the miracle he started. A few days later I returned to the hospital. Excited and expecting good news, I met the family in the waiting room as I had done the first day. Asking how she was doing I was floored to find out that moments earlier she had passed away, and I broke down in tears. It was then the family comforted me. Placing hands on my shoulders they told me how it was okay, and how this lady's passing was for the purpose of them finding Christ. Though they grieved for their loved one, they knew she was in a better place at the side of Jesus. It was a textbook answer, coming from an entire family that had just discovered salvation days earlier. It was a mature answer coming from "baby" Christians that solidified my belief their conversion was real.

In the end this experience teaches that God is concerned about a relationship with Him, and not the actual miracle, or lack thereof. If motives interfere with the relationship then more often than not the answer to God's prayer will be a denial of our own. Of course, with man's understanding of God there are no absolutes, for God is infinitely bigger and more capable than anything human kind can imagine. Paul conveyed this idea to the Ephesians in 3:20, **"Now to Him who is able to do far more abundantly beyond all that we** *ask or think, according to the power that works within us."* God will use the Christian far beyond his comprehension and request. However, as this scripture says, "the power" is within us. That power that lies within the Christian is severally inhibited not only by faith, but more often by motives. So is the lack of miracles in the modern church and indictment of the motives of its members? Yes it is. Miracles were commonplace in the early church, and should be commonplace even in the midst of modern science and medicine. The lack of miracles is an indictment of the faith Christians have. Further, it is an indictment of the church body's relationship to God. God's will is in favor of miracles when the relationship is right. God's power flows in the presence of faith that comes by hearing the word of God in an active, subjective relationship with Him. In relationships, motives are judged by the Holy Spirit. In relationship with Christ miracles occur, and the lack of miracles in our modern church is very much an indictment of both the body and its ministers.

Yet when all things are perfect there is one remaining consideration. Scripture says, "If God is for us, then who can be against us?" That opposition comes from Satan. The power of God working in man can actually come into combat with another power, namely the power of Satan.

DEMONIC INFLUENCE

For the purposes of discussion, demonic influence is going to be defined. However, proving its existence will not be a focus. The focus of this book is healing and the factors at work, not a theological discussion designed to prove or disprove demonic influence. This author relies on Solomon's wisdom that says there is nothing new under the sun to hypothesize. If there were demonic influence in biblical times, then there are demonic influences today.

Demonic influence, as it represents opposition to the healing power of God, comes in two basic forms. The first form can be described as direct demonic oppression of possession. Many Christians fear this concept, and in fear deny its existence, but all the denial in the world will not cause the truth to change. The second form of demonic influence, which is not really demonic per se, is the ability of sin to manifest in the human body as physical aliments. It is not demonic, because it comes from the free will of mankind, and Satan is not out there with temptations to distribute individually. It exists because of original sin, and because the world is a dying place.

Upon selecting the disciples, Jesus sent them on a mission, two by two into various areas of Israel. A portion of His instructions for this mission are found in Matthew 10:7-8. Here Jesus says to the disciples, *"And as you go, preach saying, 'The kingdom of heaven is at hand.' Heal the sick, raise the dead, cleanse the lepers, cast out demons; freely you receive, freely give."* The disciples did just this and found miraculous results, so much so that people were bringing the sick to the disciples and they were being healed. That was until Matthew 17, when a man comes to Jesus with a boy who was described as a lunatic. In other words, this boy had a mental issue that manifested with him throwing himself into fire and water. The father explains to Jesus in Matthew 17: 16, **"I brought him to Your disciples, and they could not cure him."** Jesus cures this boy with a rebuke that causes the demon manifesting the illness to leave and the boy to be pronounced cured.

Naturally, since the disciples had a relationship with Jesus they used this failed answer to their prayers to discover what was wrong with them. Christ describes them first as having littleness of faith, but in Matthew 17:21 gives us the ultimate reason with, *"But this kind (demon) does not go out except by prayer and fasting."*

Within the demonic world and its influences, and in the manifestation of illness, there is an unwritten rule of authority. Certain demonic influences may be able to influence all of Christianity, while others may not be able to influence Christians that practice a greater degree of holiness like prayer and fasting. Christ, in His explanation to His disciples, was using this failed prayer to grow them spiritually. Though prayer and fasting was not a part of their lives to this point, He would teach them to pray. Upon His departure from the earth, fasting would also become a normal part of their Christian regiment. The issue important to this discussion is that demons respond to authority, and depending upon an individual's spiritual authority as prescribed by God, may or may not be able to facilitate a miracle in these instances. Nonetheless, there are demonic influences out there that manifest as physical aliments. This may be in the form of insanity, as depicted above, or any other physical manifestation.

In Matthew 12:22 Jesus encounters a man in whom blindness and dumbness was attributed to a demon. Upon removal of the demon the physical aliments disappeared as well. The end result was a demon free man who could speak and see. In Luke 9:42 a demon possessed man can be seen manifesting the symptoms of epilepsy. Again Jesus' rebuke of the demon led to a complete healing of the man. Throughout the gospels there are tales of Jesus curing blind, dumb, epileptic, and insane people through the act of rebuking a demon. As with the curing of the Lepers, He did not touch them by laying His hands on them but rather spoke to the demons to create their miracle healing. The bible does not give clear instruction on how to determine if an illness is demonic or purely physical. It does not give instruction on when it is appropriate to lay hands on a person and pray for the healing or when to speak to the demon. What is clear is that Jesus did know and He knew because He was anointed with the Holy Spirit. He knew because He had a real, intense relationship with the unseen Father.

At the peak of my hospital ministry I was acutely aware of demonic activity. So much so that I lived a life of fasting from sun down to sun down every other day. It was my intent to be prepared and not have the Holy Spirit say to me, 'This kind comes out by prayer and fasting," and for me to be unable to respond. With that in mind, I received a call one day of a woman named Candice. She was in Memorial Herman Hospital Town & Country. I did not have much information, other than she had tried to commit suicide and was on life support. As I drove in my car to the hospital I asked God, "What are you going to do?" To that I heard deep in the recesses of my brain, "Cast out the demon and she will be made well."

"Whoa"… is all I could think. Once before I had heard this request, and it was a mess, to say the least. I began to beg God to allow me to see her alone. "Please Lord, no family or nurses" was all I could pray for the 45 minutes it took me to get there. Upon arriving, my request was obviously denied. In the room were the nurse, Candice's mom, and brother. My strategy was to delay. So I began a conversation with the family that lasted hours. I found out that both the brother and mother were indeed Christians. They had flown in from out of town at the doctor's request. You see, Candice had drank anti-freeze in what I learned was her 3rd suicide attempt. The anti-freeze has ravished her body. Her liver and kidneys has ceased functioning, and the doctors informed the family she had no brain activity, and that they needed their permission to remove the ventilator sustaining her life.

We went on to talk about Candice. It seems she was living with a man and had a child or two out of wedlock, which at that point were wards of the State. And I can't see that I blame the State because Candice was also a heroine addict. To me, the story could not have been more saddening. As we continued to converse, the subject turned once again to Christ, in fact her brother mentioned in passing that it was the devil trying to put the final nail in her destruction. With that comment boldness overtook me. Two or more hours into a conversation the door opened to what the Holy Spirit had spoken to me. I told the brother of what the Holy Spirit had said on the way there. I said, "God told me to cast the demon out and she would be made well, but I do not have the authority to do it. You are the spiritual authority in this situation, and you have to do it."

His reply was expected when he said, "I don't know how to do that."

I replied, "Don't worry, I will teach you and fill in any missing pieces after you pray."

Suddenly the conversation turned to a theological discussion of demons, and Candice, who had been motionless to this point, started moving her legs. At first it was thought we were imagining something but it repeated and we called the nurse.

"Nurse come look, she is moving."

To that the nurse replied, "That's normal."

And with some "over the top" medical explanation, she said that her brain was not only beyond repair, but completely inactive, accept to run her heart.

That was more than enough for me to know the time was right. I asked her brother to pray. With me on the left side of the bed and her brother on the right we placed our hands upon his sister and he began to pray. The brother spoke a simple prayer, in fact I felt the Father's pride as what amounted to a very timid, almost cute prayer came from his lips. Upon completion I said, "Father, in the name of Jesus I command this demon in Candice to leave now." Wrapping up our conversation I told them I would see them tomorrow and that I expected big things.

Tomorrow could not have come fast enough. As I walked up to the room I was stopped at the door by a nurse. Asking what is wrong the nurse told me, "The doctor is taking the breathing tube out." I could have crawled on the ceiling like Spiderman with this news. I was like an expectant father waiting on his child. Candice had been, for lack of a better term, raised from the dead. I was ecstatic, but the family was worried. It appeared that her kidneys and liver were not functioning, and she couldn't talk from having been on a respirator, so they had no idea what the brain damage was. The doctors had told them it would be extensive. So I told the brother, God does not do things half way. I will pray for her kidneys and He will finish what He started. Doing just that, I left with the commitment to come back tomorrow.

Again, the next day was a surprise. Arriving at the room I found she was gone, so I asked the nurse were she was. She said, "she's doing so well we moved her to a new room." I found it, and her brother and I shared our excitement from the day before. He told me how all her organs were working, and that she had some peculiar memory loss. She could not remember ever having tried to commit suicide, she could not remember using heroin, and she could not remember her live-in boyfriend. Beyond that, she had vivid memories of her family and every other aspect of her life. God had not only healed her body, but in removing the demon, He also removed the memory of all those demonic activities. Candice was weak at this point, and her family was tired so I promised to come back the next day.

Again the next day was a day of surprises. Walking into the room she was alone, and after formally introducing myself for the first time, it led to a rather nice discussion. In the end I had the privilege of witnessing Candice give her life to Christ for the very first time. God had literally snatched her from the pits of hell so that He could have a relationship with her. Why this demonic influence manifested in suicide is beyond reason and quite irrelevant. Whether or not sin was the cause is equally irrelevant. What is relevant is that God used this healing to bring Candice into a relationship with Him, and in that relationship her sins are remembered no more.

Though God has the ultimate healing power and authority over the demonic, He doesn't always exercise that power due to the sin in a person's life. The notion that sin can cause disease is taboo in today's society. It seems to lack common sense and fly in the face of modern science. If sin as a cause of disease does not fly in the face of modern science then certainly the concept flies in face of political correctness. Liberals scream at the top of their voice anytime the notion that HIV is a result of sexual sin is brought up. Yet it is indisputable scientific fact that the lifestyle which has created the worldwide epidemic is contrary to the prescribed Judeo/Christian lifestyle. This is in no way to suggest that God has inflicted society with HIV as punishment for their sin. But it certainly suggests that sin has opened the infected up to some very negative consequences. This argument is no different than the old Jewish law that forbids the eating of pork. Without refrigeration, eating pork could be deadly and God made a rule to preserve life. So too, heterosexual monogamy protects against the consequences of diseases like HIV. But other lifestyle choices, as they are called, produce equally damning results.

Alcoholics run the risk of liver disease; smokers run the risk of cancer. Stress runs the risk of heart disease, but what is the cause of stress? Can stress be created by greed or lust? Most certainly it can. Can the sin of compromise manifest in the body as disease? What about gluttony? There are whole lists of diseases that are the consequence of obesity. Is obesity a result of gluttony? In some cases it is. This list continues endlessly. So if sin, and/or lifestyle have the ability to afflict people with disease because of their consequences, then by necessity it must be addressed when discussing the topic of healing.

Though political winds disagree, and modern science dismisses the notion that disease can be the result of sin, this has not always been the case. When looking for modern results, referring to the past is often beneficial. The notion that sin can cause disease was recognized even in Jesus' time on the earth. In John 9:2 the disciples asked, **"Rabbi, who sinned, this man or his parents, that he would be born blind."** Why were the disciples asking who sinned? They were asking for a couple of reasons. One, they were aware of instances when Jesus healed through forgiving sins. Second, they were under the belief that sin can cause disease. Jesus answers in the following verse, "neither." So though sin was not a factor in this man's blindness, it can be a factor in disease.

Perhaps when asking the sin question, the disciples were

remembering the paralytic of Matthew 9, Mark 2, and Luke 5. After all, Christ's first statement to the paralytic is important: *"Friend, your sins are forgiven you."* If the sin was not a cause of the disease, or at least hindrance to the miracle of healing, then Christ would have had no reason to make the point of forgiveness.

Jesus very existence was to address sin. His death occurred to provide forgiveness of sin; however the sinner shared in the act with the requirement of repentance. For this reason his message is repeated in the gospels of *"Repent, for the kingdom of heaven is at hand."* Christ did His part on the cross. Mankind's part is to repent. Why? Because sin separates man from God. Sin is the hindrance to a relationship with Him. Therefore, sin must be addressed in healing. Either before, because it is the root cause of the disease, or after because the whole purpose of God's display of power is to build a relationship. If reasoning is not enough to validate the argument, then examine Jesus' attitude for those that did not repent after the healing. Matthew 11:20 says, *"Then He began to denounce the cities in which most of His miracles were done, because they did not repent."* As the whole experience of healing is to build relationship with God, sin by necessity must be addressed.

As I pray for the sick, on occasion God will have me do that very thing. I remember once praying for a man that suffered from severe allergies. As I prayed for him I saw a vision of words going into his nose. As I read those words they were a collection of minor sinful acts. What they said specifically is irrelevant. The vision did lead me to telling this gentleman that I felt the Lord had shown me that a collection of sinful compromises had manifested in his system as allergies. He said that perhaps he should watch was he does, and I answered, perhaps you should watch what you look at. In that instance the word of knowledge led the man to repentance. Whether his allergies went away, I don't know. What I do know is God used his illness for the word of knowledge to lead him to repentance so that He could have relationship with Him.

In perhaps a more dramatic instance where this was applied, I know a man through which God has healed many people. This man had a grandfather who was a real character. He spent afternoons in the bar, evenings with prostitutes, and though a good man in general, had a very destructive lifestyle and no relationship with God. In his late 70's he had a stroke that would leave half his body paralyzed for the remainder of his life. But in that remainder his family would take this grandfather to church every week, where eventually he gave his life to Christ. But to the grandson, both the struggle of his family caring for the grandfather and sadness of the situation was a tremendous burden. He wanted to pray for his grandfather and see God do in him what he had seen God do in so many other people. But the command of the Lord was clear. God had told him, "Do not pray for your grandfather's healing." I asked the grandson why he thought God would say that. He told me that God said, "Because I will heal him, and he will return to the lifestyle this has brought him from."

Sin in the ministers' life will inhibit healing, and sin in the recipients' life may cause or inhibit healing. Yet one type of sin remains for discussion. That is a sin by man against man. In Mark 11, Christ describes faith that will move mountains, and this is a wonderful thing to seek and hang onto. But this description comes with a very applicable command. In verse 25 Jesus says, ***"And whenever you stand praying, forgive, if you have anything against anyone; so that your Father also who is in heaven may forgive you…"*** The ***inability to forgive*** is a sin that will both inhibit healing and manifest itself as disease.

There was a man name Red who would attend church regularly. He was in his early 40's, and was wheel chair bound, unable to walk. He had a spinal cord injury, and it had left him a paraplegic. He was genuinely a good fellow, and after Katrina hit the Gulf Coast he went to Mississippi, in his wheel chair, to help deliver food his church had sent. So moved by the situation, he remained behind to do what he could to help. One evening a prophetess came to the church and told him that God has shown her that his inability to forgive was keeping him wheelchair bound. To prove it, she bent down and whispered Red's real name in his ear. Why Red was so secretive of his name, no one knows, but to this day, only she, he, and God know what it is. In tears he began to repent, and in days Red was walking. In weeks he returned to our church walking and testifying at the healing power of God, and the crippling power of holding on to an unforgiving nature.

If sin is separating man from God, then God will allow the consequences to create a situation where the opposite is true. One is hard pressed to find comfort in a partially paralyzed individual, unless of course, that paralysis leads to relationship with the Father. In Romans 8:28 Paul writes, ***"we know that God causes all things to work together for good to those who love Him…"*** Regardless of the physical effects, God can use anything for our spiritual good. There is not a formula for healing. But there are areas of our relationship to Him that can be positively affected in an encounter of someone in need, particularly when that need is for physical healing.

What is important is to not box God in. It is not about what type of anointing oil is available, it is not about what type of disease or aliment is at work, it is not about who is praying, and it is not about some magical words. It is about God and a relationship with Him. Not just the minister's relationship with God, but about every possible relationship surrounding the person in need.

IN THE NAME OF JESUS

I t is true that Jesus did say, *"in My name... they will lay hands on the sick, and they will recover."* But there is so much more embodied in the phrase, "in the name of Jesus." It is not the magic words of Christianity like Abracadabra is to the magician. It is an expression that Christ himself has sent the Christian in that very hour, to do the very thing that he is doing. "In the name of Jesus" is an expression that God has sent us, and its use should be in this context.

God is a monarchy, and the thoughts of democracy must be abandoned when considering how God moves. In Christ's time, and for most of recorded history, monarchies ruled the earth. If one kingdom wanted to send a message to another kingdom, they did not have e-mail; they would send a messenger. When that messenger arrived at the gate of the foreign Kingdom he would declare, "I come in the name of…" It is an announcement that the messenger is sent as a proxy for the King. So too "in the name of Jesus" can be compared. When it is invoked, it should be done so in the reverence and expectation of the proxy. Most importantly it should be done at the request of the King.

Healing is an exhibition of God's power to build relationship. To pray "in the name of Jesus" for a person's healing is to say God wants a relationship, and here is the proof by proxy. And yet this proxy follows a defined authority laid out by God. Within this authority there are defined roles, just as in any chain of command or line of authority. Even within the trinity of the Father, Son, and Holy Spirit there are defined roles, and though described in the bible, they are subjectively experienced through relationship.

1 Corinthians 12:4-6 states, *"Now there are a varieties of gifts, but the same Spirit. And there are varieties of ministries, and the same Lord. And there are varieties of effects, but the same God."* Paul was defining the roles within the authority of the trinity, and it is important to pay attention to these. Gifts such as wisdom, word of knowledge, faith, healing, miracles, prophecy, distinguishing of spirits, tongues, and interpretation of tongues are all within the role of the Holy Spirit and it is the Holy Spirit that is *"distributing to each individually just as He wills."* Therefore one must have

a relationship with the Holy Spirit to be a recipient of the gift of healing. Christ, on the other hand, has the role and responsibility of ministry. He has the role of bringing mankind into relationship with God the Father. At the same time, God the Father is the one who causes the effect. So the Holy Spirit supplies the tools, and Jesus picks the target and makes the way to the Father, but God the Father is the one ultimately at work supplying the necessary power to effect the change. Why? As verse 7 of the same chapter states, *"for the common good."*

Prayers from healing that follow this line of authority, and respect these roles of responsibility are prayers that avail. Christ determines who will receive the ministry gifts of the Holy Spirit. But in most cases the prayer needs to be directed at the Father. "Father, in the name of Jesus…" What does this say? It says, God, the creator of the universe, your Son has commanded me to minister to this person in this way. It declares the audience. The prayer might go, "Father, in the name of Jesus, I command these legs… etc." Here the object of the command is the legs. The audience is the Father, and Christ is the authority sending the message. Again, it is not the words that are magical; it is the relationship and faith behind the words.

The words describe a separate relationship with the trinity. The words acknowledge there is a difference in those relationships. This does not come from saying words. It comes from experiencing Christ, and experiencing the Father, and being filled with the Holy Spirit. This is not something that can be thought. It is something that the Father has to show you in His timing, but Christ opened the door for direct access to the Father. He is drawing each and every Christian to Himself through that door. The Holy Spirit aids in that communication. The Holy Spirit is the ISP (Internet Service Provider) of the spiritual world. In fact the Holy Spirit is the SSP, spiritual service provider.

In a monarchy the King has ultimate authority. His army has a great deal of power, but only the king has the authority to send that army to battle. In America the military possesses enough power through nuclear weapons to destroy the world. But only the President has the authority to order their launch. This distinction between power and authority must be understood as well. Power is the ability to effect a change. Authority is the ability to wield or command that power. In the case to healing, power is what causes the miracle and comes through the Holy Spirit. The authority to use that power comes through Christ. Many ministers teach that the Christian is automatically bestowed with this authority upon salvation, however 28 years experience tells me otherwise.

If a Christian has the authority to command God's power, then why are healings a rare occurrence in modern society? Certainly Christians all over the world pray for people to be healed, and yet only miniscule percentages are. Our discussion of the five factors affecting healing has shown us why, and the statistics further exemplify that the argument that Christians are endowed with authority upon salvation is false. No one could argue that apart from God, man does not have the power to heal with simple words or a touch of the hand. The power is God's. Even Christ acknowledged this, as when He taught the disciples to pray He said, *"For thine is the kingdom and power, and glory, forever."* Yet so many arguments are made concerning authority and Christianity.

One argument for authority to heal comes from the belief that like the disciples, every Christian shares in the ability to heal the sick and cast out demons. The reality is that Jesus very specifically gave the disciples authority to advertise His ministry. In Matthew 10:1, *"Jesus summoned His twelve disciples and gave them authority over unclean spirits, to cast them out, and to heal every kind of disease and every kind of sickness."* With this transfer of authority, the disciples experienced a 99% success rate of their prayers. Remember there was one person they could not heal because of the demon that could only be cast out by prayer and fasting. In another instance, Jesus transferred His authority to 70 people for the purpose of preaching the kingdom of God. They went out into the countryside, and upon their return the results of this transfer of authority are seen in Luke 10:17: ***"And the seventy returned with joy, saying, 'Lord, even the demons are subject to us in Your name."*** It was this transfer of authority that allowed the power of God to move so freely. Without that transfer of authority, modern healing miracles are dependent upon hearing the will of God, and Christ individually prescribing the use of power to accomplish the goal. Christ's authority extended far beyond healing. In His authority He forgave sins, executed judgment, and even commanded the wind and waves. In His authority, He defied the laws of physics, walking on the water and allowing Peter to do the same with Him. Jesus stated in John 10:18, concerning His very life, ***"I have the authority to lay it down, and I have the authority to take it up again."*** As the twelve disciples, and later the seventy, went out, they were not accompanied by Jesus, but they were a proxy of His authority because He had specifically given it to them.

The evidence that God heals even today far outweighs any argument against it. However, the evidence that God's authority has had a limited transfer to mankind since Jesus is certainly evident.

Authority comes individually and from above. Jesus, when confronted with Pilate's authority to release or crucify Him, responds in John19:11, ***"You would have no authority over Me, unless it had been given you from above…"*** Certainly the authority to command the crucifixion of Christ existed with only one man. The Pharisees would have done it long before had it been within their authority. And that authority was transferred from God individually.

The primary argument here is that Authority, as an ability to command God's power, independent of any other influence and in essence at the will of man, is transferred on an individual basis, and not as an automatic right of Christianity. If it were an automatic right, then the response of Peter in Acts 8:19 might have been different. There a man asks for Peter to give him authority to touch people and fill them with the Holy Spirit. He even offered to pay for it. This man already had been saved according to the passage. Peter could have responded, "you don't need to pay, it's already inside you." But instead rebukes him with, ***"you thought you could obtain the gift of God with money!"*** The authority came individually as a gift. Do not forget that gifts from heaven in the form of isolated miracles or broad authority are, as 1 Corinthians 12:11 says, the work of the Holy Spirit who is ***"distributing to each one individually as He wills."***

While on this earth Christ had authority, and it is this authority that distinguishes Him from the miracle performing prophets of old and the anointed miracle performing ministers of today. The Apostle Paul acknowledges this in Ephesians 1:22, *"(God the Father) put all things in subjection under (Christ) feet, and gave Him as head over all things to the church."* To the Colossians Paul says something very similar with *"(Christ) is the head over all rule and authority."* So if authority belongs to Christ, then it is not the Christians' simply because of salvation, but must be transferred at some point. This transfer can be temporary or perhaps even permanent. But in every case the transfer of authority is limited. If the Christian is going to succeed in being the witness of healing ministries then the ideas of authority within oneself must be confronted. Earthly authority breeds greed and contempt. Spiritual authority, if not checked by the Holy Spirit in humility, will have the same results. It is not a right to pray for the sick and see them recover. It is a privilege. A privilege that as 1 Corinthians 12:7 explains is, *"for the common good."* When a man ministers with the kingdom of God in mind, as opposed to his own kingdom, and does so in all humility as a servant, then Christ will begin to transfer authority. Until then, the relationship will be the focus, and prayers will receive sporadic results, as the five areas grow to strengthen our relationship with God.

In the absence of this God ordained authority, the name of Jesus does have power. Most Christians, particularly those in charismatic circles, all know Philippians 2:9, where it says, *"God highly exalted Him, and bestowed upon Him the name which is above every name."* It is true that the name of Jesus is above every name of disease or illness, and it is no coincidences that diseases have names. Though Christ never spoke to a disease, as is common place in today's healing prayers, His name can heal when the prayer is offered in love. Yes, there are five areas at work in every healing. Yes, God's power is manifested through the authority of Christ, but prayers offered in love can bypass these issues to produce the same miraculous results. Whether or not God has spoken specifically concerning an individual healing should in no way deter the Christian from praying for the sick. In Mark 9: 38-29 there is an example of someone evoking the name of Jesus with miraculous results. John's conversation with Jesus concerning this was, *"Teacher, we saw someone casting out demons in Your name, and we tried to hinder him because he was not following us.' But Jesus said, 'Do not hinder him for there is no one who shall perform a miracle in My name, and be able soon afterward to speak evil of me."* This man experienced the power in the name of Jesus, and Christ shows that the positive results will build and change the relationship to Him. A man may not follow Christ, but if he is a witness to the power of His name, it will create a relationship with God.

Time and time again, Christ challenged the disciples thinking concerning miracles, serving the purpose of removing the focus from man and returning it to God. In the above example John perhaps thought that he had some kind of spiritual authority because He was a close follower of Christ, and that in that authority he saw miracles performed at his hands. But Jesus was implying, "don't focus on the man, don't focus on the miracle, but focus on God." Christ was saying focus on your individual relationship to Me and not someone else's. In Matthew 7:22-23 Jesus teaches on this very principle. The principle is that it is all about an individual relationship with Him, and that the outward results are no indication of a person's relationship. Here He says, ***"Many will say to me on that day, 'Lord, Lord, did we not prophesy in Your name, and in Your name cast out demons, and in Your name perform many miracles?' And then I will declare to them, 'I never knew you; depart from me, you who practice lawlessness.'"*** This seems in direct contradiction to what Jesus said to John in the exact situation. And though it is the exact opposite, it is not a contradiction. What is important to Christ is not the miracle but the relationship.

With John, Jesus was saying, "leave him alone because he will come into relationship with me." In the Matthew teaching, Jesus is saying, "so what if you performed miracles, you had no relationship with me."

As the relationship to Christ increases, and as the Christian begins to experience and come to know Him, then miracles will naturally begin to occur. So, is the sporadic nature of healing miracles in America an indictment against the Christian body's relationship to Christ?

It could be argued that the sporadic occurrence of miracles in America is absolutely an indictment against it. In Revelation 2 John receives a message from Jesus concerning the church in Thyatira. Now this was not specific to Thyatira, but to all churches, all generations who suffered from the same symptoms. At first Christ applauds their love, faith, service, and perseverance. He applauds the godly things that are very evident in churches across America, but immediately following this compliment He then explains that the church is full of sexual sin. He describes this as tolerating Jezebel the prostitute. The consequence for this hypocrisy was to be pestilence. Could it be that miracles do not occur in churches because the pay-per-view porn rate in hotels is the highest when Christian groups check in? Could it be that miracles do not occur regularly because sexual perversions go unchecked in the form of same sex marriage and other abominations to God? Probably not, but it is possible.

If this argument were true, then surely there would be a period of time in American history where miracles were more prevalent, and there is no historical evidence to support this. The reality is that God will find a generation that will seek Him, and with humility and love pray from His miracles so that the common good of relationship to Him will be served. The question is, will *you* be part of that generation?

THE GIFT OF HEALING

1 Corinthians 12:7, ***"But to each one is given the manifestation of the Spirit for the common good."*** This passage does not make a promise that everyone will experience the power of God to heal working through them, but it does promise that every Christian will be given some manifestation for the common good. As followers of Christ, the Christian should be seeking what manifestation the Spirit will give to them individually. As this manifestation, this "gift" is sought, relationship will be established. It will cause a relationship because as the gift is sought, invariably the question of why and why not will come up. When the Christian asks God why, then God will use the opportunity to reveal the character of that individual to himself through a revelation of Himself. Out of this confrontation with our true nature and an encounter with Jesus Christ our relationship to Him is further

developed. If anything, the notion that every Christian should have some miraculous manifestation of the power of God should compel each one individually to in part measure their relationship to Him by the presence or absence of this ability. If prayers are not being answered, the Christian's next prayer of God should be, why? Invariably, the answer will rely deep in the character of the Christian. Invariably, it will be an area of the relationship to God that the Holy Spirit is trying to improve. As a Christian who has experienced God heal frequently, it is my desire to see God heal constantly and at every time the prayer of healing is offered. If the gift of healing exists, then there is a place in relationship to Christ where this gift is absolute.

Further in the same passage of 1 Corinthians, Paul names the gifts of healing. Perhaps because Paul describes it as gifts (plural) and not a gift (singular), there is not a place in a relationship with Christ that the prayer of healing is absolute. But certainly the desire to find that place will keep the relationship dynamically moving to greater and greater subjective knowledge. Regardless of whether or not absolute healing exists within the gifts of healing, the gifts exist nonetheless. Some congregations and pastors work very hard to help the Christian determine their gifts. In one of the purest intents ever experienced, Pastor Benedito in

Cordoba, Argentina explained how he wanted to know each gift of his congregation, because he knew it was for the common good, and he did not want anyone in his congregation to miss out on any manifestation of the Holy Spirit. The results of this search for the gifts within were beyond spectacular. So spectacular that they have document perhaps thousands of bonafide healings through exams by licensed practicing physicians.

In the absence of a uniformed spiritual gift test the Christian can discover their gift through prayer. For me, I knew at a very early age the gift of healing would operate through me. I can remember in high school having dreams of laying hands on people and seeing them healed. That was probably the first indication for me. A second form of indication occurred less frequently with this feeling of compulsion to pray for sick people. Early in my business career I was on a trip to Chicago for some training. As I retrieved my bags and was about to exit the airport a man in front of me collapsed from an apparent heart attack. All the while the Holy Spirit was telling me to go and lay my hand upon him and pray for him. But at that time I was in my early 20's and had never done anything like that. Fear and potential embarrassment were all I felt in response to the Lord's command, and I did not pray for him. I was more concerned about what my wife and the paramedics attending him would say than obeying the compulsion within me.

Ultimately for me there was a day and time when God actually made ceremony of presenting me with the gift of healing. I will not go into specifics for fear of contaminating your experience, but it should suffice to say that it was unmistakable. Additionally, there have been times when God has commanded me to pray for others and "share" with them the gift of healing. There is obviously no scriptural support for this, but there certainly is scriptural support for the laying of hands on to receive the Holy Spirit. It can be deduced that if the Holy Spirit can be imparted through a touch, then His gifts can be shared in a similar matter.

In the end the focus is not the gift, but rather the relationship to Christ. The gift and the subsequent manifestation are road signs in our relationship. When gifts manifest in the Christians' life for the common good, that relationship to God is increasing. But heed the warning of Matthew 7 and focus on the Giver, and not the gift. The success or failure of the prayer is never the focus. The focus is knowing Christ and knowing Him more fully. When Christians begin to pray for the sick, and when the miracle of healing occurs and increases, then the whole body will benefit in relationship.

TESTIMONIES

No book on healing would be complete with out examples of healing. Over the years I have seen God heal hundreds of people. I believe that the gift of healing operates in me for reasons previously stated. When the gift is present there are normally two things that occur in me. The first is that I am moved with a supernatural compassion. The second is that there is a physical change in a part of my body. Again, I do not want to describe this physical change because I do not want to contaminate someone else's individual experience. But for me it is completely consistent. Learning to recognize these two signs within me has been one of the simplest things God has given me, and are clear indicators to me that He is about to heal someone. The following are some brief examples of the experiences.

The very first healing that I saw God perform occurred in

Mexico. I was there on a mission trip with the ministry school I was attending. Someone brought a woman to me that had some kind of growth in her abdomen area. The growth was the size and texture of a head of cauliflower. I do not know the nature of the illness, and it could have been some kind of large hernia but the results of my prayer literally shocked me. As I laid my hand on the growth and prayed I felt it disappear under my hand. The sensation can be compared to jello being sucked through your teeth. It appeared to disappear into her body from the middle out. It was an incredible miracle of God.

There are many testimonies of healings that I witnessed on those Ministry School trips, but there is one that really touched my heart. On these trips we would go into the Colonias (neighborhoods) and invite people daily to the services at night. We had a children's service in conjunction with an adult service. As part of the children's service we would have clowns. This miracle occurred one night when I was a clown. There I was in my green wig, full costume and makeup, and standing at the rear of the service was a young woman holding a baby. It was clear the baby was afflicted with Down's Syndrome. I was completely moved with compassion. Yes, I am a father and I do have a heart for children, but this was God's compassion that I felt. I asked the woman if I could hold her baby so that she could enjoy the service. I also asked if the baby was a Down's baby, and the woman affirmed this through an interpreter. He was also blind. As I held that baby, all I could do was stare into his face and cry. There was no concern for my appearance as a clown. All I could think of was this poor woman, without adequate medical services to ever properly care for such a challenged child. Weeping, I wiped away tear after tear from my eye, and prayed to God to please heal this baby. At some point the Holy Spirit said, "allow your tears to fall on the baby." Even now, as I write this, tears flow from my eyes at the memory. So I obeyed. "What could it hurt," I thought to myself. Tear after tear fell onto that baby, in his face, in his eyes, on his forehead. And before my eyes that baby's face transformed. The best edited special effects video could not portray the transformation I witnessed as I cried on that baby. I saw God move facial structures from classic Down features to a perfectly normal looking baby.

Another time in Mexico a couple of friends and I were called to take medicine and supplies to a woman that was not mobile enough to make it to the service. Upon arriving we met an elderly person who only wanted medicine for her arthritis. Being there to minister, we agreed to give her the medicine, but we asked if we could pray for her. She agreed because she wanted the medicine, but after we prayed all the pain had left her body. She did a couple of deep knee bends in amazement and as she came up from one she lifted her shirt, exposed her belly, and said pray for this. There on her abdomen was clearly a hernia. We were confused and asked her, "why didn't you tell us about this." Her reply was because I didn't think God would heal me, I was just letting you pray to get the medicine. Like the woman with the cauliflower growth, this woman's hernia disappeared to the touch. She would then give her life to Christ, and as we left we asked her if she wanted us to leave the medicine. She replied, "No, I don't need it. God healed me."

Some people are not so thankful. I remember one trip to the VA hospital to pray for a man with a diagnosis heart blockage. I met him the day before surgery and they were planning on doing an angioplasty the next day. He was a gruff old man and not all that receptive to my visit, but I felt God's compassion, and I could feel the healing gift operation going on inside me. I prayed and told him that I would return after the surgery. Returning the next day I asked how the surgery went. He explained to me that they did the surgery, but could not find the blockage. His attitude was that of a man put out, not one who God had graciously healed. Surely at some point the reality set in, but I was not a witness to it.

If I have witnessed God heal hundreds, then I would have to

say that I have prayed for thousands. Typically I will only pray for incurable diseases unless someone is just insistent that I pray for them. In those that I have literally watched die, I would say that cancer was the number one cause of their deaths. When I found out a friend was diagnosed with cancer, I can tell you that I had very little faith to see her healing. Even still, I wanted badly to see her healing. She was a young mother, and my roommate in college lost his wife early in their marriage to the same disease. So I sought God earnestly as to His plan for her, and my role if any in her healing. Eventually I saw a vision of me pouring some anointing oil on her that I brought with me from Argentina. This oil I had purchased in the US, but I took it with me on a mission trip to Argentina. For whatever reason, I had every pastor we met pray over the oil. Over the course of the trip the oil's color changed from a clear golden to an opaque brown. Not particularly important, but I thought interesting. Upon seeing the vision I called my friend and told her I need to come and pray for her, to which she gladly agreed.

Normally ministers will just put a dab of anointing oil on their hand and pray for someone. But in my vision I saw a pouring of the oil, and not just a dab, so I had to ask her if this was ok. Her attitude was basically, I have cancer, do what you want. So I did put a handful of oil on her head and prayed. That was it. Within weeks she was diagnosed cured and remains cancer free to this day.

One of the coolest miracles I ever witnessed was for a newborn in ICU. This little girl had been diagnosed with a hole in her heart the size of a quarter and was to undergo surgery to repair it. Normally small holes will heal themselves, but this baby's mother was a drug addict and the prognosis for her was not as good. This was my first trip to the neonatal ICU, and little McKenzie was hooked to a heart monitor and under a warmer. I could see the beat of her heart on the monitor, and between the beats were a bunch of jagged peaks and valleys. I suspected that the hole in the heart was the cause, and asked the nurse to confirm my suspicion. She did, and so I laid my hand on her tiny chest, and began to pray silently. I never closed my eyes, but I could feel once again the gift of healing very strongly in me. As I watched the monitor, the noise between the heart beats disappeared. As the rhythm normalized, I lifted my hand and left. That afternoon they took her for an ultrasound in preparation of the surgery. To the doctors' amazement, they could find no evidence of the hole.

One of the more memorable times of praying for the sick happened with a man named Bob that I met in the hospice. Bob was there with full blown, incurable cancer that had metastasized all over his body. His prognosis was three days to live when I met him. As we talked for the first time, it was painfully clear that he was a practicing Christian with a full relationship with God. He had made it 70+ years through life, and had accomplished all that he has set out to. As we talked the Holy Spirit said something very new and shocking to me. He told me to tell Bob, "If he will get up and walk out the door, I will heal him." At the time I was using the standard lay hands on them and pray. But in obedience I relayed the message to Bob. Bob replied, "I feel that too." So I asked, "What are you going to do?" He answered, "I don't know." So I said not to worry about it, but think about it and I would check on him tomorrow. When I came back the next day, there was Bob, no pain, no medication, having a conversation like a man without a deadly disease. So again I asked him if he was going to get up and walk out the door. Again he replied that he didn't know yet. This went on for 3 weeks. In the third week I came to Bob and he told me that he still had not decided. He said, "Jeff, I'm not in any pain, but I had to start taking some pain medication because they were going to kick me out." This really was of no consequence to me, as I figured if God was going to extend the invitation to be healed by walking through a door everyday for three weeks, what was one more day. The very next day I heard something from Bob that I have never heard from a man. Bob told me, "I'm ready to go see Jesus. I am not walking out that door." This broke my heart, but at the same time the lesson was worth the broken heart. I left that day telling Bob I would come see him everyday until Jesus brought him home. Arriving the next day, the Bob I saw was very different from the Bob I had just seen the day before. He was in immense pain, and his mouth was full of ulcers, as in common in the final stages of cancer. We had an incredible conversation about Christ, and as I left I told him to tell Jesus I love Him. Bob replied, "He told me to tell you He knows." I left with the promise to return tomorrow. Arriving at the hospice the very next morning I told the receptionists I was going to see Bob. They told me that Bob had died the night before.

It is a rare event for me to preach. I am a minister, but by profession I am a mortgage banker. My time to pray for people comes largely from volunteering and opportunity, so when I was invited to preach in Tomball, Texas, I had to invite friends to come and hear me. Among the friends that I invited was a Jewish friend of mine. No big deal, but in the service God showed me a woman in a black pantsuit who had back trouble. After the service I called for her, and a woman meeting the description came up and God healed her. After the service I took my Jewish friend to lunch and she explained to me how she had wished she was that person. She was in a black pantsuit and unbeknownst to me, she had back trouble. We both knew it was not her but we did get the chance to discuss many things about Christianity. As we left lunch, I prayed for God to heal her as a testimony of Christ, and as I prayed and drove to my house I saw a vision of this woman sitting in a chair at my house. As she sat there in my vision, I noticed her left leg was shorter than the right. I also saw my eldest daughter who was 14 at the time praying for her. So I called her on my cell phone and told her to come to the house. Arriving there I told her to sit in the chair and as I picked up her legs to compare the sizes if was evident the vision was dead on. She asked how did I know, and I told her that I just saw it in a vision. Not only was the leg shorter, it was magnitudes smaller. Now I had to explain to my daughter that she was supposed to pray. She resisted momentarily because she didn't know what to pray, but after I explained she only need pray, "Father in the name of Jesus I command this leg to grow" she agreed. There I held her feet, suspending her two legs suspended at 90 degrees, and asked my daughter to pray. Tearfully she prayed, "Daddy God, please make this leg grow… please, please, please." Immediately the leg began to grow in my hands. About the third "please" I told my daughter, "Stop honey, we don't want it to get bigger than the other leg." My friend and my daughters were cry-ing in amazement at the power of God. I laughed with enjoyment at the lesson He had given my Jewish friend and my daughter. To this day she still has no back pain and no difference in leg size, to my knowledge.

Research in the area of the power of prayer indicates that the three most common areas where results are measurable are for hearts, strokes, and back pain. This is certainly true in my expe-rience. I have seen numerous healings in all three areas. For me it is awesome that God does heal, but I tend to look more for the indisputable healings. I prefer to pray for people with diagnosed, incurable diseases. Four times I have witnessed God open blind eyes--and there is no dispute or misdiagnosis possible when He displays His power in this manner. I look forward to the days when I see God snatch the terminally ill cancer patient from the jaws of death. Though I have seen the brain dead live, I more than anything want to see the mother with metastasized breast cancer leave the hospice under the power of God. I look forward to the day when the power of the Holy Spirit destroys HIV. I have only seen the beginning of what God is going to do in the area of heal-ing and so have you.

Acknowledgments

I have to first thank my parents for dragging me to church every Sunday of my life. It was hard to sleep on the wooden pews, but ultimately it created habits in me that would lead to coming into relationship with Christ.

Thank you, Bob Philips, for listening to the Holy Spirit, and more than supporting my writing efforts. You have my respect, my love, and my devotion as a spiritual son.

Thank you to Pastor Benedito for Patricios in Cordoba Argentina. In answering my questions you demonstrated the love of Christ, and wisdom that had to be born above. I hope to one day soon return and rekindle the friendship you have shown me.

Special thanks to Dusty Kemp who in one conversation released the Holy Spirit's inspiration for this book, and who's teachings are largely incorporated herein.

To my Pastors Mark & Laura Shook, I love you guys so much. You truly have the largest family of anyone I know, and I am so grateful to be a part of it.

About the Author

1 John 1:8-10, *"If we say that we have no sin, we are deceiving ourselves and the truth in not in us. If we confess our sins, He is faithful and righteous to forgive us our sins and to cleanse us from unrighteousness. If we say that we have not sinned, we make Him a liar, and His word is not in us."* If there is anything to say about me, the first thing would be that I am a sinner. And though I strive to not have sin in my life, I fail everyday. Yet God in His mercy and grace continues to expand our relationship and allow me to build on His relationships to others.

I do have a calling in ministry, but my first ministry is to my teenage daughters and five year old son. In that capacity I work daily to provide for them through the mortgage industry. For me life has been easy, and life has been difficult. I have felt financial security and I have literally lost everything of monetary value. In short, I'm just an average American male that God has used from time to time to convey His word and to display His power.